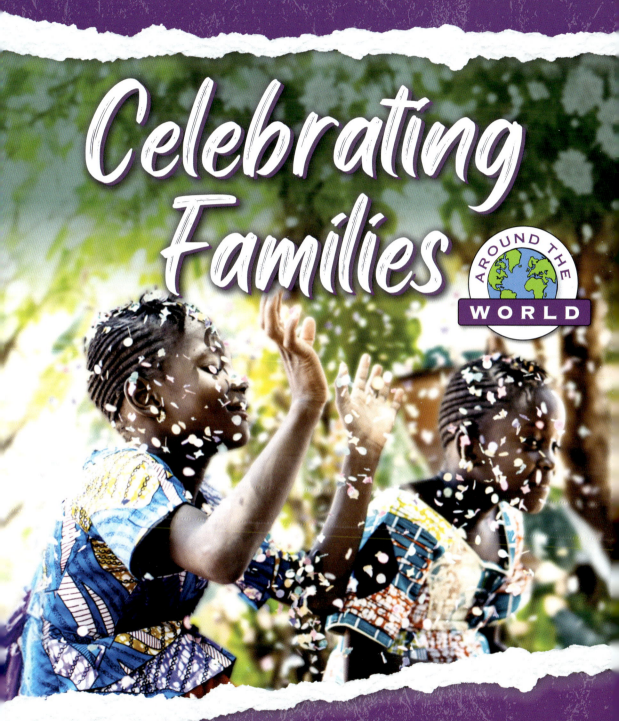

How the World Celebrates

Celebrating Families

Around the World

Jennifer Kleiman

45th Parallel Press

Published in the United States of America by Cherry Lake Publishing Group
Ann Arbor, Michigan
www.cherrylakepublishing.com

Reading Adviser: Beth Walker Gambro, MS, Ed., Reading Consultant, Yorkville, IL

Photo Credits: © Borgogniels/Dreamstime.com, cover, title page; © DNF Style/Shutterstock, 4; © taufik imran/Shutterstock, 6; © Drazen Zigic/Shutterstock, 7; © CREATISTA/iStock.com, 8; © Olena Serzhanova/Shutterstock, 10; © Fernanda_Reyes/Shutterstock, 12; © Marcos Castillo/Dreamstime.com, 14; © ASSOCIATED PRESS; © AGCuesta/Shutterstock, 16; © ferrantraite/iStock.com, 17; © PamelaJoeMcFarlane/iStock.com, 18; © nickichen/Shutterstock, 21; © Rozenn Leard/Dreamstime.com, 23; © mauritius images GmbH/Alamy Stock Photo, 24; © Kwame Amo/Shutterstock, 26; © Shutterstock; © Debbie Aird Designs/Shutterstock, 28; © Thao Lan/Shutterstock, 29

Copyright © 2025 by Cherry Lake Publishing Group
All rights reserved. No part of this book may be reproduced or utilized in any form or by any means without written permission from the publisher.

45th Parallel Press is an imprint of Cherry Lake Publishing Group.

Library of Congress Cataloging-in-Publication Data

Names: Kleiman, Jennifer, 1978- author.
Title: Celebrating families around the world / Jennifer Kleiman.
Description: Ann Arbor : 45th Parallel Press, 2025. | Series: How the world celebrates | Audience: Grades 4-6 | Summary: "Cultures all over the world celebrate and honor family members in different ways. Readers will explore holidays, customs, and traditions that show love and appreciation for the people in our lives that help make us who we are. This hi-lo narrative nonfiction series celebrates diverse cultures while highlighting how expressions of joy and connection are all part of the human experience"-- Provided by publisher.
Identifiers: LCCN 2024036507 | ISBN 9781668956588 (hardcover) | ISBN 9781668957431 (paperback) | ISBN 9781668958308 (ebook) | ISBN

Cherry Lake Publishing would like to acknowledge the work of the Partnership for 21st Century Learning, a network of Battelle for Kids. Please visit Battelle for Kids online for more information.

Printed in the United States of America

NOTE FROM PUBLISHER: Websites change regularly, and their future contents are outside of our control. Supervise children when conducting any recommended online searches for extended learning opportunities.

Table of Contents

INTRODUCTION **5**

CHAPTER 1:
AN AMERICAN MOTHER'S DAY................... **9**

CHAPTER 2:
A MEXICAN DÍA DEL NIÑO...................... **13**

CHAPTER 3:
CHINESE XIAO..................................... **19**

CHAPTER 4:
A ZULU IMBELEKO CEREMONY **25**

ACTIVITY:
CREATE A FAMILY TREE OR WEB **30**

LEARN MORE.. **31**
GLOSSARY... **32**
INDEX **32**
ABOUT THE AUTHOR **32**

DID YOU KNOW? Not all families are related by blood or marriage. A chosen family is made up of close friends. They provide love, support, and a sense of belonging.

Introduction

Family. What does the word mean to you? Maybe your immediate family comes to mind. These are your closest family members. They are usually the people you live with. Immediate family can include your parents, siblings, or other relatives or guardians. Members can be related by blood, adoption, or marriage.

Then there is your extended family. This refers to all your other living **kin**, or relatives. An extended family can consist of several generations. It can include cousins, aunts, uncles, grandparents, and other relatives.

What about your **ancestors**? They are family too. They lived generations ago. They are not alive today. They include your great-grandparents, great-great-grandparents, and so on.

Families come in all shapes and sizes. They vary by culture. In the United States, the **nuclear family** is most common. A nuclear family consists of parents and children living together. In other countries, extended families commonly live in a single house. Some tribal communities are even **communal**. Different families share a home. They also share family roles.

Family roles vary by culture too. In India, elders are the head of the family. In other communities, women are the heads of the household. They even carry on the family name. Ancestors play a sacred part of family life in many cultures.

The Minangkabau people of Indonesia are the largest **matrilineal** society on Earth. Women make family and community decisions. Property and wealth pass from mother to daughter.

6

THE ROLE OF FAMILY

Families play a big role in who we are. They shape our values. They teach us what is important and worthwhile. They teach us right from wrong. These values shape our character. They shape us as we grow.

Families also inform our identity. Our families show us where we came from. They pass down traditions and beliefs. They share our history.

Most importantly, families take care of one another. They provide love, support, and guidance. They play an important role in our well-being. Strong family relationships make us stronger. They make communities stronger too.

MOTHER'S DAY began in the United States in 1907. A woman named Anna Jarvis invented it. In 1914, President Woodrow Wilson made it a national holiday. Today, countries around the world celebrate Mother's Day. In the United States, it is the second Sunday in May.

Chapter 1
An American Mother's Day

Damiene hears his mother stirring. She is awake. He has been waiting. His father says not to wake her. Damiene knocks on the door and enters quietly.

"Happy Mother's Day," he whispers. He then places the breakfast tray on her lap.

Mother smiles when she sees him. She sits up. "You made me breakfast in bed."

"I've also written you a poem." Damiene sits beside her on the bed to read it.

> For My Mother,
>
> I wrote my mother a poem.
> I made her breakfast in bed.
> The first is to tell her I love her.
> The second will keep her well-fed.
> You always love and nourish me.
> Now it's my turn to say.
> Thank you for all that you do.
>
> Happy Mother's Day!

Damiene looks at his mother's face. It is beaming.

"No one has ever written me a poem," she says. "I love it!"

His father appears in the doorway. He's brought flowers. He wishes his wife a happy Mother's Day. He gives her a kiss.

"What do you want to do on your special day?" he asks.

She surprises them. "Absolutely nothing!"

Damiene thinks about his mother's request. He knows his mother has 3 jobs. She serves food at a restaurant. She is a student. She is also a parent. Today is her day. It is a day to honor her. Today, she has chosen to rest.

Damiene and his father honor her by granting her wish. She wraps herself in a blanket on the couch. She spends the afternoon reading. Damiene's father makes dinner. The family is quiet and respectful. They do her chores, as well as their own.

In the evening, they join her on the couch. They watch a movie together. She hugs her family close and thanks them. "This was just what I needed," she says. "Thank you for a perfect Mother's Day."

DID YOU KNOW?

Fathers also get their own day of honor in the United States. Father's Day is the third Sunday in June. It was introduced by Sonora Smart Dodd in 1909. She got the idea while listening to a Mother's Day church sermon. Smart's mother died in childbirth. Her father raised Smart and her 5 siblings. Father's Day is in June to honor his June birthday.

DÍA DEL NIÑO is a Mexican holiday. It means "Children's Day." The holiday occurs on the last day in April. It is a national celebration of children and childhood. The day is focused on making children feel loved. Family and children are highly valued in Mexican culture. The first official Children's Day took place in 1925. Other countries followed in 1954.

Chapter 2
A Mexican Día del Niño

There are no classes today. The teachers have organized a day of fun for Día del Niño. Students don't have to wear uniforms on Día del Niño. Señora Hernández passes out small bags of chocolates. They are gifts to her students.

This will be the last year Juve's class celebrates. Next year, the students start *secundaria*, or secondary school. They will no longer be children. They will be teenagers. Juve tells his friend Rogelio that he will miss the holiday.

"We are too old for 'Báte, Báte, Chocoláte,'" Rogelio says. This is a song children sing on Día del Niño. It is about making chocolate.

Juve bites one of his chocolates. "We may be too old to sing about it," he says. "But we're not too old to eat it."

The morning is filled with games and prizes. The children play *Lotería*. It is the Spanish version of Bingo. Rogelio wins first prize. He gets to pick something from the wheel of prizes. He chooses a coupon. It gives him extra free time in class.

A CHOCOLATE TRADITION

Báte, Báte, Chocoláte means "Beat, Beat, Chocolate." In Mexico, making chocolate from scratch is a common practice. The practice is often passed down from generation to generation. The song encourages children to participate in stirring the ingredients.

Later in the morning, parents are invited to school. Spending the day with family is an important part of Día del Niño. The students take turns teaching their parents simple lessons. This shows that children have valuable knowledge to share too. After lessons, parents and students eat lunch together on the patio. Juve's younger siblings join. The family eats together.

In the afternoon, the school hosts a carnival. The community has helped **sponsor** it. This means that they helped pay for it. Everyone enjoys carnival games, live music, and food. Sticky-mouthed children run around. They wave cotton candy wands.

A long line has formed at the piñata. Everyone takes turns swinging at it. One of the bigger kids manages to break it open. Treats spill onto the ground.

Juve and Rogelio play carnival games. Then they join their families for churros. The fried dough is still warm. The smell of cinnamon and sugar lingers in the air.

Dinner is at Juve's grandparents' house. The whole family is there. His *abuelita* makes dishes that she knows her grandchildren enjoy. They include Juve's favorite tamales. They are sweet and filled with raisins and coconut. He is the only one in the family who likes them. She has made them especially for him. She smiles at her grandson when she sees him eating them.

After dinner, the family plays board games. Siblings and cousins fill the room with laughter. The sound causes their grandfather to check on them.

"*Lo siento, Abuelo,*" says Juve. "I'm sorry, Grandpa. Are we being too loud?"

Abuelo smiles. "Not at all, *mijo*. A house is not a home without the sound of children."

XIAO is the Chinese word for **filial piety**. Filial piety is an important concept in China. It's an attitude of respect for parents and elders. This includes ancestors. It consists of obedience, devotion, and care. Filial piety **prioritizes** elder family members. It puts them first.

Chapter 3
Chinese Xiao

In Jing's family, love is not expressed in words. It is not traditional to say, "I love you." This is a Western tradition. Chinese parents and children do not often share emotions. Instead, they show their love. They demonstrate it through deeds.

Parents feed and take care of their children. They give them the material things they need. They take care of them when they are sick. When children grow up, the roles are reversed. They are **indebted** to their parents. They owe them for their sacrifice.

Today, Lao Lao is moving in. She is Jing's mother's mother. Lao Lao has lived alone since Jing's grandfather left this world. Normally, elderly parents live with the eldest son. Jing's mother is an only child. So Lao Lao will move in with Jing's family. This way, she will not be alone. She will have family to care for her.

Jing sweeps Lao Lao's room. She makes her bed. Growing up, Lao Lao never made Jing's mother do housework. Jing looks shocked.

Her mother explains, "It was her way of saying, 'I love you.' Lao Lao worked hard to keep our home organized and clean. She wanted me to focus on my studies. Now it is my turn to provide for her."

Lao Lao arrives in time for dinner. Jing's father drove her from Shanghai. It is a long drive. Jing greets Lao Lao first, then her father. In China, it is customary to greet the eldest first.

"*Nin hao,* Lao Lao," she says. "Hello, Grandmother." This is the greeting used to greet elders. It is polite.

"*Ni hao,* Jing," she replies. This is a greeting for younger people or equals.

DID YOU KNOW?

Filial piety is practiced in societies influenced by Confucian thought. Confucius was an ancient Chinese philosopher. Filial piety is the basis of moral behavior in China. Its influence is seen in laws, customs, and celebrations.

Lao Lao tells them about the long ride from Shanghai. They listen attentively. They wait for her to finish her story. It is impolite to interrupt.

"You must be hungry," says Jing's mother. "We have made dinner."

Everyone waits for Lao Lao to take a seat. Then they sit. Lao Lao is served first. Then Jing's parents. Then her older brother. Then Jing. Everyone waits for Lao Lao to take a bite. Then they eat.

The table is filled with sounds of slurping. It is polite to make noise when eating. It is a compliment to the chef. Lao Lao lets out a gentle burp. "It is very good."

"It is not my best," her mother replied. It is not customary to thank someone for a compliment. One must remain humble.

21

THE LAW OF PROTECTION OF THE RIGHTS AND INTERESTS OF ELDERLY PEOPLE

Filial piety isn't just a custom. In 2013, China passed a filial piety law. Part of the law explains children's responsibility to their parents. Adult children must provide support for parents who are 60 and older. This includes financial support, if needed. They must provide for their parents' basic needs. They provide medical care. They also provide culturally expected support. This includes frequent visits. It includes sending greetings. Parents can sue adult children who break the law.

China is home to the world's largest aging population. China passed this law to protect them. In Shanghai, 1 in 3 residents is 60 or older. The Shanghai government set up extra punishments for residents who break the law. They will find their name on a "credit blacklist." People on the list will have trouble with finances. This includes opening a bank account or buying a house. They will struggle to open a business. They may even have a hard time getting a library card!

After dinner, the family sits with Lao Lao. They talk about family. They discuss her younger sister, Hua. Hua's 60th birthday party is coming up. The 60th birthday is a big deal. Not much attention is given to birthdays before 60. After 60, a birthday is celebrated every 10 years. Hua's eldest son has rented a banquet hall.

Lao Lao recalls a story from her own 60th birthday. Someone had given her a clock. It came from Switzerland. It is impolite to give an elderly person a clock. It is like telling someone their days are numbered. The friend didn't know. He was foreign. He had only meant to give a nice gift. Everyone laughs while recalling the story.

It has been a long day. Lao Lao retires to her room. Jing is glad she is there. "We are lucky to have her," says her mother. "Lao Lao has a lot of wisdom to share. Listen to her. An elder is the treasure of a family."

The Chinese zodiac includes a 12-year cycle. A 60th birthday means 5 complete cycles.

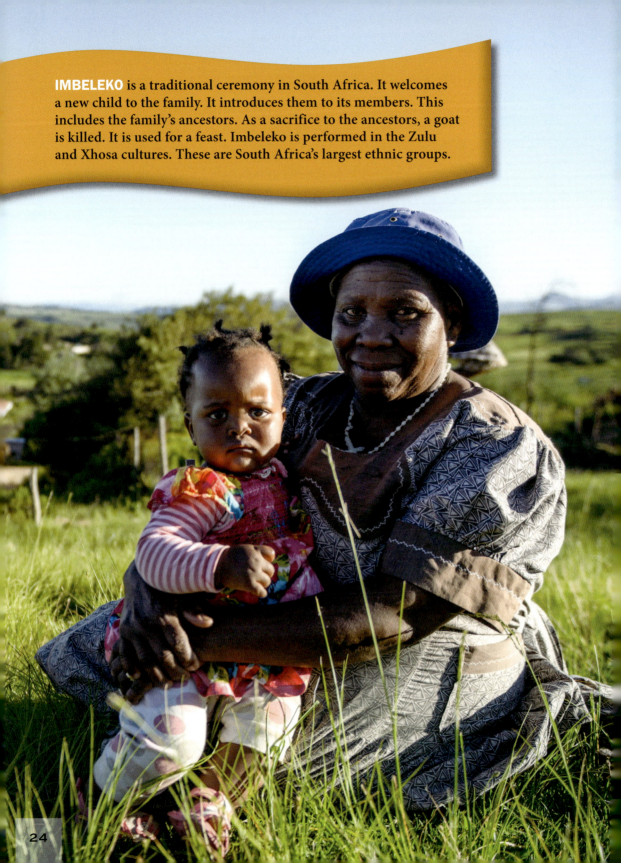

IMBELEKO is a traditional ceremony in South Africa. It welcomes a new child to the family. It introduces them to its members. This includes the family's ancestors. As a sacrifice to the ancestors, a goat is killed. It is used for a feast. Imbeleko is performed in the Zulu and Xhosa cultures. These are South Africa's largest ethnic groups.

Chapter 4
A Zulu Imbeleko Ceremony

Today, Ahmale's family welcomes its newest member. Nofoto is 1 year old, but today is her *imbeleko*. An imbeleko is an important rite of passage. Nofoto will be introduced to her ancestors. She will become a recognized family member. Without it, Nofoto will never be able to speak to them. Her words will fall on deaf ears.

The name *Nofoto* means "like her grandmother." In Zulu culture, a name's meaning is important. It is chosen before you are born. Choosing Nofoto is a gift to her *gogo,* or grandmother. It reflects her parents' hopes for who Nofoto will become. Ahmale hopes it too. Gogo is the best!

During the ceremony, Gogo will present Nofoto to their ancestors. She will call her by her name. She will ask them to protect her. Ahmale hopes they listen. She wants to keep Nofoto safe. It is her job as a big sister to help care for her. Ahmale helps Umama, her mother.

Ubaba is Ahmale's father. He has been brewing *umqombothi* for 3 days. This is a traditional Zulu beer. Brewing it is the first step in the ceremony. One of the elders must make the first offering to the ancestors. Ahmale's grandfather places a small pot of the umqombothi at the family altar.

DID YOU KNOW?

Imbeleko literally means "baby carrier." Traditionally, the skin of the slaughtered animal is used to carry the baby. The mother uses the skin to carry the baby on her back. This is how the ceremony got its name.

The impepho plant is indigenous to South Africa.

Gogo burns *impepho*. This is a sacred herb. Burning it invites the ancestors to the ceremony. Without this step, Nofoto cannot be properly welcomed.

Ahmale's father must provide a goat for the ceremony. Ubaba has given his best one. Gogo prays to the ancestors. She notifies them that the goat is here. She places Nofoto's hand on the animal's fur. This helps the ancestors connect Nofoto with the goat.

After the ceremony, the goat is brought to the altar. It is left there overnight. Different parts of the goat will be used for different purposes.

Skin from the goat's leg is used to make a wristband for Nofoto. This is called an *isiphandla*. It connects Nofoto to her ancestors, family, and customs. It also signals that Nofoto has gone through her imbeleko. It shows that she is an accepted member of the family. Nofoto will wear the bracelet until it falls off naturally. It cannot be cut without notifying the ancestors.

DID YOU KNOW?

Where is your **umbilical cord** buried? The umbilical cord connects a baby to the pregnant mother. This is a common question in Zulu culture. It is how you ask where a person is from. After birth, the Zulu bury the baby's umbilical cord. It is buried on the family's ancestral burial ground. This is the same soil where they will be buried. It is the place a person considers home.

The most important part of the goat is the bile. It comes from the liver. It is applied to Nofoto's isiphandla. This further connects Nofoto to her ancestors. The wristband will have a meaty smell for weeks. Umama dusts it with ash to lessen the smell. Ahmale can still smell it, though.

The next morning, Umama boils goat meat. Some of the organs are cooked as well. She uses the meat to make a delicious stew. Ahmale helps. She gathers the water. She takes care of Nofoto. Family and friends gather together. They share in the feast. Ahmale holds Nofoto close. Nofoto is one of them at last.

Sharing food with family and friends nourishes the spirit and the body.

ACTIVITY: CREATE A FAMILY TREE OR WEB

A family tree is a visual representation of a family's ancestry. It shows blood relationships between family members. It is often structured like a tree. You put yourself at the base. Each branch is a part of your family. Its members make up the leaves.

STEP 1: GATHER INFORMATION
- **Start with yourself:** Include your full name, birthdate, and birthplace.
- **Add immediate family:** Include your parents and siblings.
- **Collect details:** Collect names, places, birthdates, marriage dates, and death dates.
- **Interview relatives:** Gather information about extended family members.

STEP 2: ORGANIZE INFORMATION
- **Family group sheets:** Create a family group sheet for each nuclear family. Each one will be a branch.

STEP 3: CHOOSE A FORMAT
- **Paper:** Use a blank family tree template. You can also create your own on poster board.
- **Digital:** Use software or online tools to create your family tree.

STEP 4: CREATE THE FAMILY TREE
1. **Start with yourself:** Put yourself at the base of the tree. Work your way up the tree.
2. **Add details:** Include names, dates, and places for each person.
3. **Include photos:** If possible, add photos.

FAMILY WEB: A family web is a way to show important people in your life. You place yourself at the center. You put the people who take care of you around you. Add others who mean the most to you. Draw a line connecting them to you. Then talk to the people you listed. Have them add people around their own name. Connect them with lines. As your web grows, you can see the bonds of love that surround you.

LEARN MORE

BOOKS:

Hilliard, Lacey, and AnneMarie McClain. *Talking About Family.* Ann Arbor, MI: Cherry Lake Publishing, 2023.

Mora, Pat. Book *Fiesta! Celebrate Children's Day/Book Day; Celebremos El dia de los ninos/El dia de los libros.* New York: HarperCollins, 2016.

Murphy, Frank, and Alice Lee. *A Family Like Ours.* Ann Arbor, MI: Sleeping Bear Press, 2023.

ONLINE:

With an adult, explore more online with these suggested searches.

- "30 Cool Facts About China," Nat Geo Kids
- "Mother's Day," PBS Kids via YouTube
- "Zulu," Britannica Kids

GLOSSARY

ancestors (AN-seh-sterz) people from whom someone is descended; further back in the line of descent than grandparents

communal (kuh-MYOO-nuhl) shared by all members of a community

filial piety (FIH-lee-uhl PIE-uh-tee) attitude of respect and obedience toward parents

indebted (in-DEH-tuhd) owing gratitude or recognition to another person

kin (KIN) a group of people with common ancestry

matrilineal (maa-truh-LIH-nee-uhl) societies based on the maternal line

nuclear family (NOO-klee-uhr FAM-lee) a family group consisting only of parents and children

prioritize (prye-OR-uh-tyez) to list or rate in order of importance

sponsor (SPAHN-ser) a person or organization who pays for an event

umbilical cord (uhm-BIH-lih-kuhl KORD) a cord arising from the navel that connects the fetus with the placenta and allows nutrients and waste to pass through it

INDEX

ancestors, 5, 6, 7, 18, 24, 25–29, 30

birthdays, 23

Children's Day, 12–17
China, 18–23
chosen family, 4
Confucian thought, 20
cultural differences, 6, 19, 21, 22

Dia del Niño, 12–17

elders, 6, 18, 19–23, 26
extended family, 5, 6, 30

family roles, 6, 18–22
family trees, 30
Father's Day, 11
filial piety, 18–23
food, 9, 13, 14, 15, 16, 21, 29
friends as family, 4

grandparents, 5, 16, 19–23, 24–25, 26–27

identity and values, 7, 18–23, 24–29
imbeleko (South Africa), 24–29

immediate family, 5, 6, 30
Indonesia, 6
isiphandla, 27, 29

laws, 22

matrilineal structure, 6
Mexico, 12–17
Minangkabau people, 6
Mother's Day, 8–11

nuclear family, 6

parents, 5, 6, 7, 8–11, 15, 19–23

respect, 10–11, 18–23
rites of passage, 25
roles in families, 6, 18–22

South Africa, 24–29
support, 7, 19, 20, 22

United States, 8–11

values and identity, 7, 18–23, 24–29
xiao (China), 18–23

Zulu people, 24–29

ABOUT THE AUTHOR

Jennifer Kleiman has worked in educational publishing for more than 20 years. Today, she is a busy writer and editor, working on her second novel. She lives in Chicago, in a rickety old house, with her wife, 2 cats, a dog named Helen, and a yard full of chickens.